THE PROBLEM WITH BELIEVING GOD

A PERSONAL GUIDE TO INCREASE YOUR FAITH

GREGORY BRAD CUTLER

authorHOUSE®

AuthorHouse™
1663 Liberty Drive
Bloomington, IN 47403
www.authorhouse.com
Phone: 1-800-839-8640

First published by AuthorHouse 2/18/2011

ISBN: 978-1-4567-3954-6 (e)
ISBN: 978-1-4567-3953-9 (dj)
ISBN: 978-1-4567-3952-2 (sc)

Library of Congress Control Number: 2011901907

Printed in the United States of America

Any people depicted in stock imagery provided by Thinkstock are models, and such images are being used for illustrative purposes only. Certain stock imagery © Thinkstock.

This book is printed on acid-free paper.

All Scripture quotations are taken from the King James Version of the Bible, unless otherwise indicated.

Cover and layout design by Gregory Brad Cutler.
Photography by Dwight Berry of 2dphotography.

Also by Gregory Brad Cutler

IF WORDS COULD SPEAK:

When I can't find the words to say...

THOUGHTS KEEP FLOWING:

If You Were to Ask Me What I'm Thinking

WHO WE ONCE WERE

For more information visit:

www.gbcutler.com

INVOCATION

Heavenly Father, I pray – in the name of Jesus – that for every reader of this book, your Spirit will be invoked. And as each page is turned, I pray that their faith is increased. I believe, dear God, that there is no shortage of miracles in the shed blood of your Son, Jesus. So I ask now, that you would miraculously transform these pages into an anointed canvas and cause the power of your Word to spring forth, fall on good ground, and take root. In a world where the mechanics of believing defy the rules of logic, I pray that men, women, boys, and girls will be compelled to surrender their lives to you. And for every person who picks up this book, I pray that you would trouble them until their faith pleases you. For every soul that shall be redeemed, and for every heart that shall be encouraged, I give you praise. In Jesus' name. Amen.

Acknowledgments

To my Lord and Savior Jesus Christ, whose blood redeemed me into a relationship with the God who makes every opportunity possible and who does all things well.

To my family, who love, respect, and support me; and who entreat me as the "gift" that God gave to them. Thanks for embracing me the way you do and for reminding me that my "assignment" spans multiple generations and transcends family ties.

To all of my nephews, nieces, great-nephews, great-nieces, and godchildren, my love and prayers go further than you are able to comprehend.

To my aunts Queenie Cutler and Florence "Catherine" Boone, you have taught me more about faith through your actions than many could ever teach me with their words.

To the newest love of my life, my "granddaughter" Jocelyn Nicole Robinson, you constantly remind me that God is still on the throne.

To my pastor and co-pastor (Marvin & Veda McCoy), thank you for your prayers, support, and encouragement. Thank you for entrusting me with a part of the vision that God gave to you and for enabling me to carry out part of the vision that He has given me.

To my Judah Christian Center Church family, I'm strengthened by your prayers.

To my friend and brother, Elder Bobby Dunmore, thank you for always listening and laboring in the gospel with me. In times gone by, we would have been Paul & Silas or Peter & John.

To Bishop Alfred Owens and Co-Pastor Susie Owens, thank you for more than 25 years of parental oversight and support.

To Dr. C. B. Akins and First Lady Akins (First Baptist Bracktown - Kentucky), you encouraged me more in one weekend than some have in a lifetime. I've never forgotten you.

To my friend and brother, Minister Earnest Pugh, while sharing your gifts with the world, thanks for being a sounding board and encouraging me on this project.

To Bishop Earl Wortham, thank you for providing spiritual counsel as I struggled with completing this book.

To my Howard University friend and schoolmate, Dr. Dwight Berry, thank you for lending your photography skills to give me a new look.

To everybody back home in Arapahoe, NC; Pamlico County; and eastern N.C.; thanks for always believing in me.

To all the people – some who now sleep – that taught me to love God, even as a youngster. May your seed forever produce fruit.

To all the pastors and churches who opened your doors, pulpits, and hearts. Thanks for giving me a chance.

To all the people who said, "Pray for me," or "I'm praying for you." Thanks for reminding me about the power of prayer.

To all the people who are honest enough to confess that they have struggled with believing God. May God honor your honesty and increase your faith beyond measure.

To every person who will read this book and will dare to give God a devoted life and watch Him work out His plan. May you soon discover that God is thinking about you RIGHT NOW!

DEDICATION

To my mother:

Annie Elizabeth Boone Cutler

You forever remind me that God's hand is upon my life. And in so doing, you encourage me to acknowledge Him in all of my ways and to take courage in knowing that He shall direct my path. For all of those times when I struggle with knowing my purpose, thank you for reminding me to "stay in the struggle." And thank you, Mama, for staying in the struggle with me. I love you immeasurably.

To my spiritual father and mentor:

Bishop Alfred A. Owens, Jr.

If I could have chosen to be anybody's spiritually conjoined twin, it would have been you. Your example of how to live a balanced life, nestled around the core of righteousness, has been exemplary. Thank you, Bishop, for over a quarter-century of guidance and instructions in righteousness. Thank you for continuing to speak destiny over my life – perhaps even unbeknownst to you – in the midst of my seasons of emptiness and despondency. Thank you for your support on my previous book, your encouragement on all of my endeavors, your feedback on this book, and your obedience to God whenever He has directed you to call me or just cover me in prayer. You have been to me what Barnabas was to Paul. You have always spoken into my life, and I have no doubt that I am better for the day that I met you in Locke Hall, on the campus of Howard University, in 1983.

PREFACE

For I bear them record that they have a zeal of God, but not according to knowledge.

(Romans 10:2)

My earliest introduction to and concept of God, was as the One who spoke the world into existence by the mere power of His voice. He was the One who parted the sea and made dry land appear so that the children of Israel could escape Egyptian bondage. It was He who delivered Daniel out of the lions' den and delivered the Hebrew boys out of the fiery furnace. It was He who added years to Hezekiah's life and spoke to young Samuel in the still of the night. Stories about His son Jesus suggested that He could walk on water, restore sight to the blind, feed the multitude, cast out demons, turn water into wine, heal the diseased, and cause the dead to come back alive. My earliest recollections of God and His son Jesus were those of heroes who performed fairy-tale like feats; and these monumental feats seemed more like the rule, rather than the exception. Therefore, when I first became a

Christian, I had an overwhelming expectation that God could and would answer my prayers, as long as I possessed faith in His ability to do what I had asked Him. I had such zeal to live for God, and I wanted everyone else to receive the salvation that I so ardently advocated. I prayed for the salvation of family members. I prayed for the healing of the sick. I prayed that the homeless would be given homes. I prayed that the poor would strike it rich. I prayed that addicts would recover. I prayed that gifts would manifest out of nowhere. And I prayed that the oppressed would be delivered. I wanted God to do everything that I could possibly imagine.

How disillusioned I was, when my first, second, third – and eventually innumerable – prayers went unanswered! How distraught and disappointed I became when my years of faithfulness and service to God seemingly yielded very little in comparison to the young life that I had sacrificed for the cause of Christ. I had devoted my entire life to God – uncompromisingly so – yet there were simple things that I had asked of Him, things that went unanswered and sometimes seemingly unacknowledged.

But at the point when I thought about "calling it quits," I realized that my relationship was too valuable to end without venturing into some introspection and self-discovery. And in my own quest, I came face-to-face with what I dubbed as the **problem with believing God**.

During my introspection, what I re-discovered was that for every question, God has an answer; for every conflict, God has a resolution; and for every problem, God has a promise. Join me on my personal journey, as I re-visit the solution to the problem with believing God.

CONTENTS

FOREWORD

In a day when the when the Body of Christ seems to endure countless attacks from the enemy's camp, it is unfathomable to imagine that someone from within the Body would rise up and author a book with the words "problem," "with," and "God" in its title. To me, they sound oxymoronic and grossly contradictory, so if anyone were going to launch such an accusation, my prayer was that it was not someone that I had called "son" for over 25 years. As a pastor and bishop, I have heard believers talk about problems in their homes, problems on the job, problems at school, problems with the church, and even problems with other believers; but I had never heard the words "problem" and "God" used in such proximity. But then again, neither had I ever heard of "Arapahoe" until I met Elder Gregory Brad Cutler.

When I first met Gregory, he was a young mild-mannered teenager on Howard University's campus. An English minor at the time, he would assist me with grading papers, during my tenure as an instructor in the English department. He soon joined Greater Mount Calvary and began to work in ministry. He was intelligent, relatively quiet, well-organized, and gifted with handling administrative matters. He assumed leadership roles within the Music Ministry and executed his responsibilities with much dedication. He served as the assistant director and vice president of the Alfred Owens chorale, the president of the United Voices of Calvary, and the secretary/treasurer of the entire Music Department. A trip to his hometown and home church in Arapahoe, NC revealed that his humility and modesty were genuine. When he left the DC area and pursued his law degree in Atlanta, he maintained his "son-ship" and would always adjust his calendar if Co-pastor Susie or I were preaching in the Atlanta area. On a few occasions, he even prepared home-made meals and hosted lunch or dinner for Co-Pastor Susie. I was the bishop, but I guess I didn't merit the dinners. It has always been clear to me that Gregory loves God and the people of God. His life has been marked with favor, and I celebrate the blessings of the Lord upon his life.

What I was relieved to discover as I perused this book was that Gregory immediately disavows any notion that there is a "problem with God," but rather he focuses on the issues that an individual has in his efforts to believe God. He places the proverbial "problem" in the reader's lap, allows the reader to self-examine his own issues, and empowers the reader with a simplistic tool that leads to an exponentially increased level of faith. His use of the acronym "FACE" makes it easy for the reader to heighten his level of God-consciousness and walk in the will of God. From the title to the introspective questions to the personal testimony, "The Problem With Believing God" is insightful. It doesn't seem to castigate those who are weak in their faith; rather it seems to be an obedient response to the scripture in Galatians 6:1 that says, "if a man be overtaken in a fault, ye which are spiritual, restore such an one in the spirit of meekness."

Belief – or faith – is the key component in the arsenal of any individual who strives to communicate with, serve, or please God. It builds the foundation upon which religion is developed, and it creates the springboard from this life into the next. Without it, we roam aimlessly through this life leading a very temporal existence. But our belief gives us hope that there is a reward for a devoted, disciplined life – hope that "there is a crown of righteousness, which the Lord, the righteous judge, shall give" (II Timothy 4:8).

In this, his fourth book but first faith-based work, Gregory takes us back to basics and challenges us to examine our own faith to see if we understand the process of believing. It is clear that he has sought wisdom from God to ensure that the reader "gets it" and walks away with a clear understanding of the lesson that is taught through this Bible-based and scripture-enriched book. The blessing of this book is that you will walk away, not focusing on any problems, but on the promises of God. For everyone who reads this book, I am prayerful that their faith is increased, their joy is restored, the devil is defeated, and their commitment to the cause of Christ is solidified.

Gregory, my son, I am proud of you; and this one is for the Kingdom.

Bishop Alfred A. Owens, Jr., D.Div.
Pastor, Greater Mount Calvary Holy Church
Washington, D.C.

International Presiding Prelate
Mount Calvary Holy Church of America, Inc.

PART I

HELP MY UNBELIEF

CHAPTER 1

AN AUDIENCE WITH GOD

... let your requests be made known unto God.

(Philippians 4:6)

If you are reading this book, it is quite likely that you were intrigued by the title, which seems to suggest that believing God does not come without its own set of challenges. Perhaps you – like countless others – have found that there were times when you thought your faith and your belief were where they should be, yet when tried by life's storms, the results of your faith seemed empty and barren. And in desperation you may have asked yourself, "Why in the name of all that is holy, has God chosen not to respond to my prayers, my belief, or my acts of faith?" And though your lips would never utter the words, your heart, your mind, and – more significantly – your reality would suggest that there is a **problem with believing God**.

If this scenario seems even vaguely familiar, then I invite you to take a journey that explores critical issues that have the potential to cripple our faith and spiritually paralyze our belief system. And in the event that this scenario does not reflect the current status of your life, I encourage you to read this book with the mindset of empowering yourself so that you can strengthen others for whom this scenario may be a reality.

Perhaps you were raised in a family, culture, or environment that does not embrace the existence of the traditional Christian view of God. Or perhaps your experience with religion – or your experience with those who call themselves "believers" – has jaded your willingness or ability to believe in an omnipotent God who loves us, redeems us, and calls us to a disciplined life. And, finally, perhaps your quest for a well-balanced life leaves you desirous of something that fulfills your need for spiritual wholeness. Perhaps there is an emptiness, or a void, inside you that has yet to be filled by your life's journey thus far. Perhaps you are still struggling with trying to define your purpose in life. All of these experiences would lead you to conclude that there is indeed a **problem with believing God**.

The problem with believing God could very well stem from the fact that we do not always know what to believe or how to believe; and sometimes "not knowing" causes us to wrestle with whether we should even bother to believe at all. But this guide is carefully and prayerfully written and designed to help jump-start your faith and cause you to obediently respond to the scripture that says: *"Have faith in God"* (Mark 11:22).

If we are to actively engage in the process of increasing our faith, we must start with a candid introspection of where we are in our current level of faith. In other words, we have to be honest with where we are along our faith journey. Do I believe as I should? Or am I weak in faith? No one can look inside us except us and God; therefore, we must make a personal assessment and either admit or deny that our faith is – or is not – where it should be. If we fail to first look inside and make an honest self-assessment, we are destined to travel a road of self-imposed lies that lead to a defeated end.

It is critical that we are honest in our self-assessments. As Paul told the Romans, we must evaluate ourselves honestly, or *"think soberly, according as God hath dealt to every man the measure of faith"* (Romans 12:3). Otherwise, if we are not honest, the sad truth then becomes that our faith journey was of no effect, and our lives will have failed to glorify God. For *"without faith it is impossible to please God..."* (Hebrews 11:6).

As we openly address **the problem with believing God**, we must first come to a confession of who God is. Logic refutes Him. Math cannot calculate Him. History cannot adequately track Him. Language does not accurately define Him. Art does not completely depict Him. Science cannot explain Him. He just is! And the confession of our faith must begin with that very basic notion: God is. *"For he that cometh to God must believe that he is..."* (Hebrews 11:6). In other words, we must come to the realization and acceptance that there is a ubiquitous God. We must accept that God, existing in three persons – the Father, the Son, and the Holy Ghost – created all things. *"All things were made by him; and without him was not any thing made that was made"* (John 1:3).

We must believe that the same God who breathed into the first man imprinted Himself onto the soul of mankind; and He is the same God who continues to be the source of life today. It is connectivity with Him – and Him alone – that brings us to a healthy and whole life. Acknowledging this is the first step of our faith.

Then at the core of our faith, we must believe in the omnipotence of God as a problem-solver. Without that very basic premise, all else is rendered void and insignificant. So as we progress through this guide and along the quest to increase our faith, let us – as a starting point – accept, without reservation, that God is all-powerful and can do anything.

In order to better understand the power of this God that we now believe, let us consider a "sky is the limit" type of scenario where we can clearly see God's infinite power in action. Just for a moment, suppose that you have been given a personal audience with God – face-to-face – where you are sitting at the foot of His throne and He gives you an opportunity to "put him to the test." Quite frankly, this scenario is no different from the invitation that God extended to the prophet Jeremiah. *"Call unto me, and I will answer thee, and show thee great and mighty things, which thou knowest not"* (Jeremiah 33:3).

In light of such an "exceeding an abundant" invitation, what are the top five things for which you would ask God? Don't be shy and don't be afraid. This is your opportunity to put God to the test. He has given you a personal audience with Him, and has allowed you to ask anything that your heart desires – whether it is for Him to heal a sickness, cure a terminal illness, remove the physical manifestation of a crippling disease, send deliverance, save a loved one, reverse a curse, rid the world of hate or hunger, break the stronghold of certain proclivities or addictive behavior, give sight to someone who you know is blind, cause a deaf friend or relative to hear, bring a loved one to a level of spiritual enlightenment, give you peace, restore your joy, cast out demons, raise the dead, grow your personal ministry, or prosper your life. WHATEVER the case may be, you have an opportunity to "talk it over" with God.

As you sit in the presence of the almighty God and ponder what you should ask Him, perhaps your doubt is so overwhelming until you refuse to believe that God is going to do what He says He will do. Perhaps, you will require proof or confirmation, just like the scripture where Hezekiah asked Isaiah, "How will I know that the Lord has healed me from these boils on my body? What will be my sign?"

The Bible suggests that God is not always offended by such a request for proof from one who does not possess a fully matured faith. In fact, Isaiah said to Hezekiah, "You tell me what proof or indicia you would like for God to give you. Do you want the shadow on the sun dial to go forward by ten degrees or backwards by ten degrees?"

Hezekiah thought it over, and said, "It's easy for the shadow to go forward by ten degrees because that simply means the sun is going down. But it would be a hard thing for the shadow to go backwards, because that would suggest that God is reversing the normal rotation of the earth." With that said, Hezekiah asked for the shadow to go backwards. It seemed as though he was really putting God to the test. However, the Bible says that the prophet Isaiah called upon the Lord, and the shadow went backwards by ten degrees (II Kings 20:7-11).

Many of us, like Hezekiah, fail to fully accept an act of God as that. We are quick to attribute our "good fortunes" to luck, chance, our own strength, or even the actions of others. And we fail to realize that God specializes in doing things to prove Himself – those things that should leave little doubt in our minds and those things that should provide us clear and convincing evidence that He can do anything except fail. Unlike those of us who have the luxury of transferring fault elsewhere or blaming others if our efforts are futile or if our words do not manifest, God is not afforded such luxury. In fact, scripture seems to suggest that God is keenly aware of Himself as the final authority. Hebrews

6:13 puts it like this: *"because there is no one greater for Him to swear by, God swears by Himself."* He knows that the buck stops with Him; and what a wonderful testament of our faith, if we too would only believe that He is the ultimate and final source of power and authority.

Hezekiah's story teaches us that God is not necessarily offended when we ask for confirmation of His acting on our behalf. On the contrary, in some instances, it shows a heightened level of faith – to the point where we believe that not only is God capable of meeting our needs; but He is also capable of removing the vestiges of doubt that once ensnared us.

So now, because you acknowledge that He is the all-powerful God and final authority, go ahead and make your list. Ask God for whatever you want; and be sure to include those things that you might not even be able to discuss with friends and family.

1. What are the top five things you want God to do?

_____

_____

_____

_____

_____

2. Have you ever asked God about these things before?

_____

_____

_____

_____

_____

3. If not, why not?

_____

_____

_____

_____

4. If so, what – if anything – seemed to be God's response?

_____

_____

_____

_____

_____

CHAPTER 2

TRUE CONFESSIONS

... Lord, I believe; help thou mine unbelief.

(Mark 9:24)

5. *And when Jesus was entered into Capernaum, there came unto him a centurion, beseeching him,*

6. *And saying, Lord, my servant lieth at home sick of the palsy, grievously tormented.*

7. *And Jesus saith unto him, "**I will come and heal him.**"*

8. *The centurion answered and said, Lord, I am not worthy that thou shouldest come under my roof:*

but speak the word only, and my servant shall be healed.

10. *When Jesus heard it, he marveled, and said to them that followed, **"Verily I say unto you, I have not found so great faith, no, not in Israel."***

13. *And Jesus said unto the centurion, **"Go thy way; and as thou hast believed, so be it done unto thee."** And his servant was healed in the self-same hour.*

(Matthew 8: 5-8, 10, 13)

From the earliest days of our lives, we are taught to believe, and conversely we are taught not to believe. An infant who cries is taught to believe that his cry will garner the attention of a parent or caregiver who will soon come running to address his needs. A toddler who learns to walk is taught to believe in the strength of his new-found ability to balance himself on two legs even though he clumsily moves across the room with a certain amount of trepidation. An older child is taught to believe – or not to believe – in the Tooth Fairy, the Easter Bunny, or Santa Claus. A teenager or young adult is taught to believe that studying hard will yield a fruitful job and budding career. A middle age member of the work force is taught to believe that wise financial investments will secure a comfortable post-employment life. The elderly are taught to believe that the government, family, or social programs will provide for them and afford the comforts and necessities of life during their latter years. Without fail, our belief system is formed, developed, and even shaped throughout our entire lives.

We believe in dreams! We believe in love! We believe in miracles! We believe in God! We even believe in belief! We often hear, "I believe that all things are possible if I only believe." We sing about belief; we write about belief; and we preach about belief – all because we were taught that it is RIGHT to believe. We are taught WHAT to believe. However, the most ironic realization in my experience with Christendom – and even life in general – is that little to no effort is given toward teaching HOW to believe. We are taught how to read, how to write, how to walk, how to talk, how to sing, how to pray; but when it comes to a life experience that is predicated solely on faith and a belief system, it seems almost totally illogical that we would be left on our own without any concrete and readily apparent instructions as to HOW to believe. In the outset, let me say that ***I do not believe that God's word is void of instructions as to how to believe***. Rather, it is my experience that this very basic instruction set has been under-emphasized by those who are responsible for spiritual mentoring and disciple-making.

We are taught that the act of believing will rescue our own lives and can even save the lives of those for whom we activate our belief. But what good is it to be told WHAT to believe; yet left alone without refinement as to HOW to believe? For example, we are told to believe that God is a healer, a deliverer, and a miracle-worker. However, without clear and precise instructions about how to increase our faith, we are like a fish that dies on the shore when the ocean is just a few inches away. This has been much more of a reality than many Christians have been willing or able to admit. We flounder about on dry land – choking on our own disbelief, making excuses to pacify our doubt – when we could be swimming in an ocean that nurtures our beliefs, causes us to experience the wonders of God, and gives us the kind of testimony that says not only is God "capable of doing" but He is "actively doing" things in our lives.

Without this kind of "belief-enriched" life, we never experience the healings, deliverances, and miracles of a God who declared that He "changes not" (Malachi 3:6). When we do not understand the importance of belief and faith – and then compound that with the lack of succinct instructions that teach us "HOW TO" believe – we are ill-equipped for the spiritual warfare for which the armor of God is designed to prepare us. It is the "shield of faith" that makes us *able to quench all the fiery darts of the wicked"* (Ephesians 6:16). Without faith, we fall prey to all of the trategic maneuvers of the enemy, including deception, thievery, temptation, persecution, opposition, and accusation. So if we do not understand the importance of faith; and if we do not understand HOW TO activate our faith, we are destined to lose the battle. This guide is therefore designed to help increase our faith and move us from the shores of doubt and disbelief into the oceans of faith and belief, where we become empowered disciples, fully clothed for the journey and the spiritual warfare, where *"we wrestle not against flesh and blood..."* (Ephesians 6:12).

If we are to increase our faith, let us be reminded – from Chapter One – of the survey and the honest introspective look at our current level of faith. How much do we believe God? And can we identify any flaws in our personal belief systems?

Allow me to share a very candid confession of the flaws in my own belief system and to demonstrate how life can obstruct and thwart our abilities to believe in the very God whom we profess to love and serve.

For five months, I sat in a hospital with a friend who negotiated the corridors of life and death like the Greek hero Theseus, who methodically meandered through the ancient labyrinth. This friend navigated the halls of intensive care, critical care, pneumonia, dialysis, blood transfusions, a semi-comatose state, a body that was swollen twice its normal mass, a malfunctioning liver, weakened kidneys, and insufficient lung capacity. However, in what I believe to be God's response to a fervent commitment to fasting, praying, hoping, trusting, and BELIEVING, he walked out of that hospital – having literally defied the hand of death. And because of the manifestations of WHAT he believed, he possessed a renewed spirit and commitment to the God of his salvation. He was not alone in his strengthened belief and increased faith. I, along with a myriad of family and friends, was reassured through this miracle that there was absolutely nothing too hard for God. For I had fasted, prayed, diligently sought God on his behalf, and did according to the scripture that says, *"What things soever ye desire, when ye pray, believe ..."* (Mark 11:24).

I was thoroughly convinced that the response to the rhetorical question: *"Is any thing too hard for the Lord?"* (Genesis 18:14) was uncontrovertibly "No."

Nine months after that miracle, I was having dinner with another friend on the Sunday before Presidents Day. He had a lingering cough, so I suggested that he go see his doctor. In comparison to my previously mentioned friend, this friend appeared much healthier and certainly much more optimistic about his road to recovery. Having just watched the hand of God miraculously move on behalf of my other friend, my faith in God and belief in His healing power were exponentially increased and completely un-compromised. This situation with the lingering cough, I surmised, was nothing for God to handle in comparison to what I had witnessed some months earlier. In a hospital approximately six miles from the previous hospital where I had sat, here lay another opportunity for me to exercise my strengthened belief. A week passed, and then two, but this was nothing; what were two weeks compared to the five months that I had spent visiting the other hospital on an almost daily basis? My belief in God as a healer still resonated from what I had witnessed less than a year previously; and I was sure that my testimony of another miraculous healing was just around the bend. My reality, however, was that my second friend ultimately succumbed to his health challenges in just three weeks. He died on a Tuesday, was memorialized in Maryland on Thursday, and was buried in Georgia on Saturday.

I was numb; and I searched the recesses of my soul to determine what, if anything, I was suppose to have learned about the faith that I had vowed to maintain and about the belief that I had sworn to uphold. Why did God, whom I had served for the greater part of my life, seemingly disregard all of my efforts to prompt Him to move – not on my selfish behalf but – on behalf of a friend, who like the servant in Matthew 8, lay "grievously tormented" by his physical condition? What was the difference between my belief and that of the Centurion in the eighth chapter of the Book of Matthew? And perhaps the more poignant question – and the one that pierced my soul – was this: In the battle against sickness, death, and disease; were those ailments prevailing because of a flaw in how I believed? Were they wreaking havoc in my spiritual warfare? And more painfully, was my friend's untimely and premature death partially attributable and due to MY failure to believe? In other words, did I fail in my efforts to please God?

In both situations, I had fasted, prayed, and studied the account of the Roman Centurion in Matthew 8:5-13. I believed that God was a healer, but perhaps I did not believe in a manner that prompted God to heal. I believed that He was a miracle-worker, but somehow my faith did not activate the miracle working process. Apparently, I had not believed enough! My belief was now in one place, but my reality was elsewhere. And how would I come to reconcile the two? One friend was alive and the other was dead, and the accounts of this scripture plagued my mind, as I under-went a personal epiphany that I had a **problem with believing God**.

My true confession: Guilt and defeat wounded my soul; and for many months, I silenced my wounds with tears and masked my pain with make-shift praise. And to complicate matters even more, I had acknowledged the call to ministry; but how would I ever preach with conviction about faith in an area where I was challenged? But-for the Holy Ghost of God, I almost vowed never to believe God again in the areas of sickness, healing, and disease.

Consider now some of your own prayers and God's response (or seemingly lack thereof) to your requests. And as painful, angry, tearful, or despondent as you might become; take a moment to confess and trust that God is waiting – at this very hour – to hear the secrets of your heart. **If God has spared your life to get to this point in this book, I am convinced that He wants to hear from you** – the real you, who may have been masking your pain, shame, or disappointment with your own self-prescribed coping mechanisms. He wants to hear from you – with all of your doubt and fear. This is not the time to regard iniquity in your heart or to decide to just "keep it to yourself." While God knows all things, He still wants to hear from you; for He is *"touched with the feelings of our infirmities"* (Hebrews 4:15).

1. List some examples of times when you have prayed for one thing, but the outcome was the exact opposite of your prayer request.

_____

_____

_____

_____

_____

2. List some examples of times when you have prayed for something and the outcome was exactly what you had requested.

_____

_____

_____

_____

_____

3. What, if anything, do you think was the difference between your prayers in Questions 1 and Question 2?

_____

_____

_____

_____

4. Write an affirmation that expresses your commitment to seek instructions from God.

_____

_____

_____

_____

_____

5. Write a short note to God, seeking forgiveness for not always fully accepting His sovereignty.

_____

_____

_____

_____

_____

CHAPTER 3

FACE-TO-FACE
WITH MY FAITH

8. *We are troubled on every side, yet not distressed;*
   we are perplexed, but not in despair;

9. *Persecuted, but not forsaken; cast down, but not*
   destroyed;

(II Corinthians 4: 8-9)

11. *They overcame him by the blood of the Lamb and*
    by the word of their testimony;

(Revelation 12:11)

Perhaps by the time you reach this point in this guide, you can honestly confess that you possess some modicum – some small amount – of faith; and that you indeed believe in God. In other words, when asked: "Do you have faith in God?" your impromptu and immediate response is: "Yes."

But rather than simply asking, "Do you have faith," let's explore the purpose of your faith and where it leads you.

"Faith" comes from the Greek word "pistis" and the Latin word "fides" or "fidere", which translate into the word "trust." That is where we get the word "confide." It could be argued that the primary purpose of faith is to yield a life that pleases God by confiding – or having confidence – in God (Hebrews 11:6). And if we juxtapose Hebrews 11:6 with Romans 12:3 which declares that *"God has dealt to every man the measure of faith,"* then we must conclude that God has given every man the ability to trust Him and the potential to lead a life that pleases Him.

He may have granted us free will, but when our personal and selfish will lead us away from God, it can be argued that He has poured into us the substance that would point us back to Him. Some scholars could argue that it was mankind's ignoring this magnetic "substance" that caused the fall of the human race. In other words, ignoring the part of us that draws TO God actually repelled us FROM God. However, even with the fall of mankind, God in His infinite wisdom allowed us to retained the very thing that would potentially point us to Jesus and provide us with another opportunity to enjoy a restored relationship with the Father. This "faith" – or ability to believe – has to be harnessed and properly nurtured because improper nurturing would render dire consequences. Since we all retained the ability to believe, it is critical that our belief reaches proper maturation. Otherwise we possess an un-developed faith or stifled belief; and we must strengthen or develop it to a point where it pleases God. Perhaps it is the lack of developing our faith that eventually led to the founding of various religions; for they all believe in something.

But for many persons, **the problem with believing God** requires that we not just merely believe something. Rather, we must actively engage ourselves in the process of growing in the grace and knowledge of God the Father and the Lord Jesus Christ. This requires a deliberately disciplined and dedicated life, committed to maturing through God's word. Growing in faith is brought about by hearing God's word (Romans 10:17). Therefore, the more we hear and consequently believe, then the stronger our faith becomes; and the more we please God. The very poignant question then becomes: "How much am I pleasing God?"

This question brings you face-to-face with your faith, and may very well reveal that there is something lacking in your life. Maybe you find yourself vacillating and pondering as to whether or not your faith pleases or displeases God. Do you have the kind of faith that guides your life? Do you have the kind of faith that yields a fully victorious and abundant life? Are you actively and consistently committed to hearing God's word so that you please Him more and more each day? Does your level of faith make you to be at peace with all of the vicissitudes and uncertainties of life? Do you consistently speak well of God and do as we are admonished in Hebrews 10:23: *"Hold fast to the profession of your faith without wavering..."* For where there is no firm conviction, there can be no firm grasp.

All too frequently, when we come face-to-face with the confession of our faith, the truth of the matter is that although we have SOME faith, there is yet room to grow. When we face our faith, if we are honest, quite often we don't like what we see. We fail to put our faith in action. We fail to discipline ourselves according to God's will for our lives. And we fail to realize that the real victory of faith is not in getting God to do something. However, the real victory is often in the revelation of who God is and how we then choose to handle God's response to our prayer or God's lack of action towards our request. We struggle and try to differentiate between whether God CAN, as opposed to whether God WILL. Just because God did not do as we wanted, that does not make Him any less powerful or capable of doing what we asked. This was a pivotal lesson taught by the Hebrew boys in Daniel 3:17. They said, *"...our God whom we serve is able to deliver us from the burning fiery furnace..."* One part of their conviction spoke to the fact that God will; however, the first part of their conviction said that God can – that He is capable of doing it.

This suggests that even if I ask God to do something and He doesn't, then I must still accept the sovereignty of who God is. I am not skilled enough in the art of negotiation to coerce God to act on my behalf if my request is outside of His will. Either He is moved by my faith, or He isn't. And regardless of the outcome, it behooves me to embrace His decision and not exacerbate, or worsen, my situation by not accepting God's permissive will. Somehow, I must be determined to see God's hand in all that concerns me. For example, if God allows trouble to come my way, then I must be thankful for not being distressed. If He allows me to become perplexed, then I must be thankful for not being in despair. And if He allows me to be persecuted or cast down, I must be thankful for not being forsaken or destroyed. I must see His hand moving on my behalf in all matters – even in death. If I ask Him to spare my life, yet he allows death, I'm determined to see Him in victory on the other side and say, "I am no less convinced of who you are, and I still believe that you could have." Even where death is concerned, the Bible tells us that *"death is swallowed up in victory"* (I Corinthians 15:54). So then, the exercise of my faith – and the reward thereof – transcends this present life. Faith must be a lifetime endeavor. Likewise, the revelation of who God is – must unfold on a daily basis. For as long as we are in the flesh, we are incapable of comprehending the totality of who God is. But thanks be to God that there is a day coming *"when he shall appear, we shall be like him; [and] we shall see him as he is"* (I John 3:2). Fully redeemed and completely transformed into an incorruptible and immortal being, I will know Him in the power of his might and in the totality of His "God-ness."

But until then, we can never underestimate the power of blind faith, and we MUST learn how to activate our faith when facing life's situations. So for the next few chapters of this guide, let us focus on how we face life's circumstances. Do we face life in a manner that strengthens our faith; or do we face life in a manner that leads to inevitable defeat? It is my experience that life is the maze, or the labyrinth, that presents me with countless opportunities to hear God's word, speak God's word, grow in faith, please God, and overcome the enemy by the words of my testimony (Revelation 12:11). But if I cower in fear and opt to refrain from speaking about God's power – if I never confess anything – then nothing is what I can expect.

You must never allow life's conditions to dictate how much you will believe God. You must believe with your heart and not based on the conditions of the day. *"With the heart man believeth..."* (Romans 10:9-10). God never fails the person who puts his/her trust in Him. We must strive to have the kind of faith that will get Jesus' attention; and we must be careful because there are two things that will cause Jesus to marvel at us – either our faith or our doubt. In Matthew 8:10, He marveled at the Roman centurion's faith. *"When Jesus heard it [the confession of this man's faith], he marveled, and said to them that followed, 'Verily I say unto you, I have not found so great faith, no, not in Israel.'"* However, in Mark 6:6, after He had cast out demons, healed the woman with the issue of blood, and raised the 12-year-old girl from the dead, the people mocked him and *"he marveled because of their unbelief."*

As we move into the remainder of this guide, it becomes necessary to ensure that Jesus is marveling at us – not because of our unholy life, but because of our righteous living; not because of our back-biting and gossip, but because of our love for our fellowman; not because of our self-righteous and judgmental attitudes, but because of our fervent prayers for all mankind; and not because of our doubt, but – because of our faith.

As we transition to the remainder of this guide, if you are serious about increasing your faith and leading a life that pleases God even more, then ask yourself this simple question: "What is my approach – my attitude, my mindset, my disposition – when facing life's situations?" Or simply put, "How do I face life?"

Consider two acronyms for the word "FACE;" and ask yourself whether you face life with

Fear, **A**nxiety, **C**onfusion, and **E**xcuses;

or do you face life with

Favor, **A**uthority, **C**onfidence, and **E**xpectation?

One approach is destined to lead to increased faith, victory, and a life that pleases God. The other should cause you to conclude that the **problem with believing God** stems from how you face life, and should encourage you to "PUT ON A NEW FACE."

Fear, anxiety, confusion, and excuses are all natural responses of the flesh to a challenging situation or to an issue that takes us out of our comfort zone. They cripple, paralyze, weaken, and distract us from focusing on purpose, destiny, and God's divine plan for our lives. Therefore, we must remember that it is up to us to crucify the flesh daily. (Romans 13:14 & Galatians 5:24-25). We are less inclined to succumb to sinful and fleshly responses if we empower ourselves with the Word of God. In other words, we cannot give our flesh what it wants, because if we feed our flesh, then in essence we are starving our spirit. So then, we must take the opposite approach and starve the flesh and feed the spirit, so that when the flesh responds with fear, we can walk in favor; and when the flesh wants anxiety, we can walk in authority. It is this daily crucifying of the flesh that leads us to actively believing God.

Let us now make an accurate assessment of our faith.

1. On a scale of 1 to 100, what percentage of your life do you believe pleases God?

_____

_____

_____

_____

_____

2. When you come face-to-face with your faith, are you actively engaged in behavior that you know displeases God?

_____

_____

_____

_____

_____

3. What would it take to move your life to a place where your life pleases God more than your response to Question 1 above?

_____

_____

_____

_____

_____

PART II

HOW TO BELIEVE

(Put on a new "FACE")

Fear   **F**avor

Anxiety   **A**uthority

Confusion   **C**onfidence

Excuses   **E**xpectation

PREAMBLE

"GOD'S FACE"

And God said, Let us make man in our image, after our likeness ...

(Genesis 1:26)

There are many people who are without hope, peace, strength, joy, healing, and deliverance. These people are looking to the church – the body of Christ – for answers, but if the believers don't believe, then non-believers don't stand a chance. For *"if the righteous scarcely be saved, where shall the ungodly and the sinner appear?"* (I Peter 4:18) It is the righteous who are called to be the "salt of the earth" and a "city that sits on a hill." It is the righteous who represent the face of God in the earth. And when the world looks at – and looks to – the righteous, they need and want to see the face of God.

When Peter and John were at the gate called "Beautiful," and Peter told the lame man to "look upon us," they were not standing in their own strength. Yes, they initially wanted to bring the man's attention to the fact that they were mere mortal men, but they shifted his attention and urged him to look beyond their mortality and to look into the face of God. That is when Peter spoke to the man "in the name of Jesus Christ of Nazareth" and commanded him to "rise up and walk." (Acts 3:6) If the lame man would have never been invited – as it were – to look into the face of God, then arguably he might never have been healed.

So then, since we are created in the image and the likeness of God, it is our responsibility to resonate **God's voice** when people hear us. It is our responsibility to extend **God's hand** when people touch us. It is our responsibility to replicate **God's heart** when people call on us. And it is our responsibility to show **God's face** when people see us.

Chapter 4

Walk In Favor

(not in fear)

11. By this I know that thou favourest me, because mine enemy doth not triumph over me.

(Psalm 41:11)

7. For God hath not given us the spirit of fear; but of power, and of love, and of a sound mind.

(II Timothy 1:7)

One of the most crippling, debilitating, and even paralyzing emotions – and certainly one that is most detrimental to a fulfilled life of walking in ones purpose – is fear. Among the factors that impede our ability to believe God, fear seems to rank high on the list. In some instances, fear can be considered an asset; however, when fear distracts us from walking in the favor of God, it becomes anything but an asset.

The Bible speaks of two types of fear; and when navigating the tides of life, it seems quite apparent that we should embrace one and shun the other. When the Bible speaks of the "fear of the Lord" as the beginning of wisdom (Psalm 111:10), this kind of "fear" is synonymous with the Greek word "eulabeia" which means "reverence." More specifically, it suggests that we should take diligent care to recognize the presence of God. This kind of fear brings us into a healthy relationship with God and enhances our ability to worship, trust, and honor Him. Therefore, this type of fear should be encouraged and embraced.

However, the complete antithesis of this reverent kind of fear is the "spirit of fear." The spirit of fear causes timidity, intimidation, and doubt. One of the problems with believing God is that when we face life's challenges, we sometimes face them with fear, instead of with favor. This kind of fear has some of its roots grounded in the notion of losing. We are afraid that if we verbalize the things that we are believing God to do – and they don't come to pass – then we will lose. Lose our reputations, lose our status, lose our credibility... But the truth of the matter is that rather than facing hurdles with fear, we should face life walking in the favor of God.

Our relationship with God cannot be muddled with fear. God is love and "perfect love casts out all fear." (I John 4:18) We have to walk in the confidence and knowledge that God loves us and that He has our best interest at heart. God does not want us to be afraid; He has not given us the "spirit of fear." (II Timothy 1:7). Rather, He has given us love, power, and soundness of mind – so much so until the strength of my relationship with God will cause me to see through His eyes and know the thoughts that He has for me. At that point, I can stand in the favor of God and believe God to work on my behalf. I will know His will for my life; and I can invoke His hand to move in my life. And if, by chance, I verbalize something that does not come to pass, then my relationship with God keeps me with a sound mind, knowing that because He loves me, He's doing what's best for me. So... rather than losing anything, my mind is so sound until I focus on the fact that my relationship has been preserved because of favor.

And I don't have to worry about losing my reputation. I don't have to be afraid that I'm going to look bad or that God is going to look bad. I don't ever have to worry about defending God's reputation. I'm too feeble to defend His reputation. In Genesis 22:16 and Hebrews 6:13, God declares that He can defend His own reputation. He says that because there is no greater power, He can take an oath in His own name. What greater favor to walk in, than in the favor of His majesty – and in the power of His sovereignty!

That's what the whole scenario with the Hebrew boys was all about. (Daniel 3) They weren't afraid to verbalize what they believed. And they were not afraid that God would not do what they said. They told the king: "We will not bow down. God will deliver us, And even if He doesn't, it's not Because He can't, so we still won't bow." Simply put, they knew that either God would or He would not. And that should be our guiding principle: Either He will or He won't. And if He doesn't, He's no less God; I'm no less His child; and my faith in Him is no less – period!

The "spirit of fear" feeds my doubt, but the favor of God fuels my belief. Fear says that I'm pre-occupied with the notion of losing; but favor says that I walk in the knowledge of who God is. And this requires no more than a mind-shift. **We have the power and the capacity to shift our lives from fear to favor.** Proverb 3:3-4 says that we should never let mercy and truth leave us. But if we tie them around our neck and write them on our hearts (display them outwardly and inwardly), then we will find favor in the sight of God and man. And the fact of the matter is that the truth of who God is, is not contingent upon the challenge that I'm facing. I may have undergone a near-death experience, may have buried my closest friend or loved one, may have been diagnosed with a life-threatening illness; but none of that can change the truth of who God is. I can try to re-create myself every day, but I can never re-create God. God is always God. And He's always omnipotent. And He's always ubiquitous. And He's always able. And He's always wonderful. The truth of who God is will NEVER change. God's power and sovereignty will never diminish or be curtailed because of anything or anybody. And if we consciously and consistently command ourselves to walk in the knowledge of that basic truth, then we implicitly activate the favor of God. You can speak to yourself and say: **"I command myself to walk in the knowledge of who God is. God is my righteousness. God is on my side. And God has my best will at heart."** It is at that point along life's journey when God's gives special regard to our condition and entreats us with exceptional kindness. When we obtain His favor, He shows us mercy (see Psalm 119:58); He responds to our requests (see Esther 7:3); and He prevents our enemies from triumphing over us (see Psalm 41:11).

Fear says that God is going to forsake me. Favor says that "God is committed to me." He's committed to seeing me through. He's committed to blessing me. He's committed to delivering me. He's committed to making a way for me. He's committed to making things work together for my good. He's committed to leading me in paths of righteousness. He's committed to perfecting everything that concerns me. (Philippians 1:6) **"I command myself to walk in the knowledge that God is committed to me!"**

God's favor should not be misconstrued as a mechanism to get everything that we want. We don't walk in the knowledge of who God is simply to get "things." Instead, I walk in the knowledge of who God is because it sustains my mind, gives me peace, and keeps the devil under my feet.

My attitude must now dictate that I don't cower in the limitations (fear) imposed by the enemy, but I bask in the omnipotence of God. I've got God's attention, and I walk in "favor."

1. Describe/identify some of the things that fear had prevented you from asking God.

    _____

    _____

    _____

    _____

    _____

2. Write a personal statement about how you plan to decrease the level of fear in your life.

    _____

    _____

    _____

    _____

    _____

3. What strategies will you take to constantly remind yourself about the truth of who God is?

_____

_____

_____

_____

_____

4. Describe/identify some things that you want God to commit Himself to doing on your behalf – or simply because you ask Him?

_____

_____

_____

_____

_____

5. Having moved further from fear and closer to favor, what old or new requests will you now present to God?

_____

_____

_____

_____

_____

CHAPTER 5

STAND IN AUTHORITY

(not in anxiety)

"But God, who is rich in mercy, because of His great love with which He loved us, even when we were dead in trespasses, made us alive together with Christ (by grace you have been saved), and raised us up together, and made us sit together in the heavenly places in Christ Jesus."

(Ephesians 2:4-6)

Cast all your anxiety on him because he cares for you.

(I Peter 5:7 – NIV)

Whenever an individual is born, adopted, or married into a certain family, he is granted the authority to use the family name and to enjoy the privileges associated with it. One of the more disappointing behaviors that a child, a sibling, or a relative of any kind can exhibit is that which is inconsistent with how the family has come to be known. Likewise, when we – as members of the Body of Christ – behave or believe contrary to the standards of the family, we reject our God-given right to stand in the authority of Jesus, and we ultimately bring reproach on the Body of Christ. When an individual fails to acknowledge the grace and the favor that has been bestowed upon his lineage, he accepts a standard of living that is incongruent with God's plan for his life. His decisions – be they spiritual, social, psychological, financial, or emotional – all become inconsistent with the authority that has been granted to him. Perhaps even Jesus himself, if He would have never acknowledged that He was the son of God, the theophany, the visible manifestation of God, or God in the flesh; He might never would have performed miracles or died on the cross.

Whenever one is granted "authority," he is endowed with an innate ability to make certain decisions, based solely on who he is. We must understand that God places us in the Body of Christ so that we can access the power of Jesus' blood and the authority in His name.

In the building up of our faith, we must walk consciously in the knowledge that we are the children of God. "Beloved, now are we the sons of God..." (I John 3:2) We were created in His image and His likeness (Genesis 1:26-27). And though we may have been separated from Him because of our sins, whenever we accept Jesus as Lord and Savior, we are spiritually re-born, re-created, and "RE-AUTHORIZED" to call upon His name with an assurance that He will act on our behalf.

Yes, we have authority THROUGH THE NAME OF JESUS. "Wherefore, God has also highly exalted him, and given him a name which is above every name." (Philippians 2:9) **We are God's masterpieces** (Ephesians 2:20) **and we have to walk in the consciousness of not only who God is to us, but also who we are to God.** We are joint-heirs with Christ; and we are spiritually exalted because of Him. *"But God, who is rich in mercy, because of His great love with which He loved us, even when we were dead in trespasses, made us alive together with Christ (by grace you have been saved), and raised us up together, and made us sit together in the heavenly places in Christ Jesus"* (Ephesians 2:4-6).

God has created us and specifically placed us hierarchically in his creation with domain and authority. "What is man that thou art mindful of him...For thou hast made him a little lower than angels, and have crowned him with glory and honor" (Psalm 8:4-5).

God has given us an assurance, that when we belong to Him, we are no longer in anxiety, but we are in His will. (Matthew 6:25-34). And when we are in His will, we don't have to have anxiety (long-term worry and nervousness) about bills, grades, jobs, food, sickness, crises, health, image, opinions, impressions, or anything else. We don't have to have anxiety over whether or not He hears us or whether the devil will defeat us. God has given us authority because of the name and the blood of Jesus.

Anxiety is counter-productive to our ability to believe God. It is a waste of precious time, and it wears at the soul. (Proverbs 12:25). It distracts us from our ability to effectively pray and have peace. (Philippians 4:6-7). And it causes us to believe that God does not care for us. (I Peter 5:7).

Believing God requires that we walk daily in the realization of our authority – standing in liberty (Galatians 5:1) and without condemnation (Romans 8:1) and – without anxiety. We have to constantly remind ourselves that we are not poor, pitiful, and pathetic; but we are powerful and authoritative. We abide in the shadow of Him who has all things under His feet!

1. Describe/identify some of the things that have recently caused you to worry or have anxiety.

_____

_____

_____

_____

_____

2. Explain how you think God feels about your worries and anxieties.

_____

_____

_____

_____

_____

3. How do you respond (physically, spiritually, and emotionally) to worry and anxiety?

_____

_____

_____

_____

_____

4. Instead of worry and anxiety, what might be a healthier and spiritually enriching way for you to respond to obstacles, challenges, and hurdles?

_____

_____

_____

_____

_____

CHAPTER 6

WALK IN CONFIDENCE

(not in confusion)

God is not the author of confusion.

(I Corinthians 14:33)

Cast not away therefore your confidence...

(Hebrews 13:6)

One of the most erosive vices used by the enemy is confusion. Confusion typically comes about whenever two or more entities are at odds with each other; and quite often it causes disarray, lack of clarity, lack of understanding, chaos, disagreement, division, or disorder. Although confusion is often characterized as disagreement between two entities, it can also occur within one individual. For example, it is not uncommon for an individual to be conflicted within his heart, mind, or soul about ideas, thoughts, philosophies, opinions, or beliefs. This type of confusion plagues the believer and inhibits him from standing confidently in the knowledge of God. Confusion, with respect to the Body of Christ, takes place in the minds of believers; and can only be dismissed in the presence of knowledge and understanding. In the battle for our minds, the enemy is cunning. He is not always overt. Rather, his strategies are often subtle and crafty. He wants to interfere with our love for – and confidence in - God. As believers, we must be so ever mindful that one of the enemy's greatest attacks is on the very thing with which Jesus told us to love Him – our mind. When faced with the question of "how to inherit eternal life," Jesus' response was simply to "love God with all your heart, soul, strength, and mind." (Luke 10:27) It seems logical that the enemy would therefore wage war for our minds. We must realize that confusion is an attack on our mind. But God has given us a prescriptive remedy, that if we keep our minds on Him, he will keep us in perfect peace. (Isaiah 26:3) What we need more than anything is God's peace – confidence in God's absolute authority.

"God is not the author of confusion." (I Corinthians 14:33) Confusion is spawned by the enemy when he presents the believer with options that fly in the face of God's plan for our lives. Options – in and of themselves – are not bad, but they become destructive when they interrupt our confidence in who God is. For instance, there is nothing wrong with logic; however, when logic becomes an option for – and opponent of – faith, it erodes our confidence. Likewise, there is nothing wrong with wealth and riches, but when wealth and the love of riches become the top priorities of life, they too erode our confidence.

Confusion clouds judgment, distorts reality, and blurs the ability to fully see how God is working on your behalf. It is the enemy's subtle means of interrupting a harmonious relationship that is based on the confidence that God honors His word. At the core of all spiritual confusion, the enemy imposes a battle of the wills – self-will versus God's will – and removes the confidence that says: "God knows what's best for me."

God, through His word, admonishes us to be single-minded with a focused confidence in Him. We see this in both the Old Testament and the New Testament. In I Kings 18:21, Elijah reminded the people that they could not be halted between two opinions, but rather they had to stand confidently in God rather than Baal. In the New Testament, James 1:8 reminds us that we cannot waver and have faith at the same time because "a double minded man is unstable in all his ways."

The Bible clearly reminds us that we should not be conflicted or confused as to whether or not God will act on our behalf. Hebrews 13:6 urges us to "say with confidence, 'The Lord is my helper…" (New Living Translation) Philippians 1:6 says that we can be "confident that he who began a good work in [us] will perform it…" Confidence is the state of mind where there is assurance and no doubt. Confusion would cause one to vacillate between assurance and doubt, but confidence dispels doubt. If we are going to believe God, we must stand boldly on the notion that God WILL respond to our requests.

We must not throw away our confidence in God (Hebrews 10:35); and we must always exhibit more confidence in God than we do in man. (Psalm 118:8) In our quest to believe God, there should be confidence about God's stance concerning man, His stellar creation. We can take confidence in God's ability and in His love. He has the power to do "exceeding and abundantly" (Ephesians 3:20); and He loved mankind so much until He sent His only son to redeem our relationship with Him (John 3:16).

We must be confident enough to know that regardless of our current situation, God is working on our behalf; and sometimes, all He's trying to do is increase our faith in Him. No matter how bad it looks, His intention is to build our faith and cause us to stand confidently in His ability. For example, when Lazarus died, it seemed illogical to some that Jesus did not rush to be with his friend during his impending illness. Rather, He remained where he was until Lazarus died. Then He told his disciples, *"I am glad for your sakes that I was not there, to the intent ye may believe"* (John 11:9). He was trying to build their faith, and wanted them to stand confidently in the knowledge of what they knew He was capable of doing.

It stands to reason therefore that our faith is strengthened when we walk in the knowledge of God's power and love. This clearly is an act of our will, which we must rehearse daily – to the point where confidence becomes second nature.

Confidence, therefore, is an act of our will. It allows us to "speak those things that are not, as though they were" (Romans 4:17). We can choose to be confused; or we can choose to be confident. We can choose to become an open target for the fiery darts of the enemy, or we can choose to stand as a yielded vessel for God. The choice is ours! We can choose to believe the lies of the enemy, or we can stand confidently on the Word of God, filled with promises. His Word reminds us of the regard that He has for His creation; gives us an assurance of who He is; and allows us to take confidence in the fact that if we give Him a devoted life, that He will order our steps and cause all things to work together for our good.

1. Describe/identify a recent moment of confusion that challenged your confidence in God. What were the two competing thoughts in your mind?

_____

_____

_____

_____

_____

2. During your last moment of confusion that you described above, which of the two competing thoughts seemed most compelling?

_____

_____

_____

_____

_____

3. Moving forward, whenever you have moments of confusion, how will you determine which thought comes from God and which thought comes from the enemy?

_____

_____

_____

_____

_____

4. Write a personal statement that honestly expresses your confidence in God's ability to hear and answer your prayers.

_____

_____

_____

_____

_____

CHAPTER 7

LIVE WITH EXPECTATION

(not with excuses)

If I didn't believe that He could, I wouldn't expect that He would.

-- Gregory B. Cutler

Excuses have been around as long as mankind itself; and unfortunately they have seemed to be indicative of behavior that reflects poor judgment or disobedience. In Genesis 3:6-12, Adam and Eve disobeyed God, discovered their nakedness, and then tried to hide from God. And when God questioned Adam, he blamed the woman; and when God questioned Eve, she blamed the serpent – excuses! For the average individual who fails to do what he should have done, making an excuse seems to be a natural inclination and reaction of the flesh.

Making an excuse is essentially a method of offering faulty rationale to mask poor judgment for certain decisions and behavior. For those who walk in the flesh and have little to no sense of spiritual awareness, making excuses may become a coping mechanism and socially acceptable behavior. However, for the believer, making or living with excuses is far from "socially acceptable." It robs the believer of joy, causes a disruption in peace, and challenges the believer's faith by creating a dichotomy between what "should be" and what "is." In other words, living with excuses involves a battle between the flesh and the spirit. It entails more than just diverting attention away from an inadequacy, an improper response, an inappropriate behavior, a less than ideal outcome, or a flaw in ones character.

The danger in living with (or habitually making) excuses is that when we accept excuses as the norm, we compromise a life that consistently glorifies God; and we risk taking advantage of the mercy and grace of God (Romans 6:1). Many times excuses are by-products of direct overt disobedience to God's word; and we have to be careful not to resurrect the very thing – sin – that we have died to (Romans 6:2). For example, when God's word says that we should believe, trust, honor, follow, study, pray, fast, refrain, flee, praise, worship, give, comfort, feed, etc.; then we have to be careful not to allow a response such as, "I'm too weak; I'm too tired; I'm too busy; I'm pre-occupied; I just can't do it; I'm too sleepy; or I'm not comfortable with that," to lead us back into a place of direct disobedience to God's word and His will for our lives.

When it comes to excuses, the enemy is cunning and will try to convince us that as long as we are telling the truth, then no harm can result from what we say. However, excuses are not necessarily un-truths, or lies. Nonetheless, they are still counter-productive to the will of God. How? Because they cause us to give other things priority over the will of God. In Luke 14, Jesus taught the parable of the man who made a great supper and sent his servant out to bid others to come; but they had to tend to the land, take care of animals, and attend to a spouse. What they said may have been true, but the crucial point to recall is that in Exodus 20:5, God told us that He is a jealous god and that He does not tolerate anything – or anybody – being given priority above Him. There is certain danger in trying to make God play second fiddle to anything.

When a believer lives with constant excuses, he walks in doubt of who God is and what God is capable of doing. He is continuously plagued with the notion that goals are unattainable and expectations are unachievable. He fails to understand why God does what He does and why God allows what He allows. The danger in this respect is that the believer puts himself in a position of trying to judge what God should have done. Quite frankly, the enemy wages war in the mind of this individual who – without exercising wisdom – might potentially compromise his expectations of God's abilities, drown in self-condemnation, or become judgmental. He lacks conviction and harbors the inability to completely accept the will of God, as well as forgiveness from God.

When we don't have a firm conviction about the strength of what we believe (and live with excuses), we give the enemy an in-road to challenge us about any and everything. We defeat the enemy, however, when we are "fully persuaded" about the expectation of what God is capable of doing. We must be convicted that God can do anything and that He stands poised to answer our prayers. If our faith is to be strengthened, then we must walk in the expectation that "what things soever we desire when we pray" if we believe, then we shall have them (Mark 11:24). The Biblical reference for "expectation" is "hope;" and the Bible admonishes us to hope in God (Psalm 42:11).

There is a distinct correlation between faith and hope. Faith is the substance of things that are hoped for (Hebrews 11:1). In other words, the things that I expect God to do are derived from what I know He can do. To take it one step further: If I didn't believe that God could, I wouldn't expect that He would. And somewhere within our souls we must resolve that God is "able to do exceeding abundantly above all that we may ask or think" (Ephesians 6:20).

We should never let the enemy force us into an uncompromising situation where we feel as though we have to make excuses for an outcome that God allows. For instance, when the thing I want to happen does not happen, I don't have to make an excuse for God. God swears by His own name (Hezekiah 6:13). He IS – and always will be – the final authority. And just because an outcome does not line up with my expectation, that's no reason for me to lose heart. It becomes my responsibility to determine whether my expectation lines up with the will of God. And if my expectation does not line up with the will of God, then I must seek God's guidance, through prayer and through the study of His word, so that I will know what to expect; because the expectations of the wicked will perish, but the hope of the righteous brings joy (Proverbs 10:28).

As believers, we don't have to give anything else priority over God and we don't have to offer any faulty rationale for our disobedience to God. Instead, we should live with expectations of what God is capable of doing; this includes forgiving us if we "come clean" and confess our sins (I John 1:9). And by all means, we must reject the enemy's accusations toward God.

The enemy would contend that God should have done a whole lot of things. He should have healed me. The cancer should have dried up. The illness should have left my body. He should have blessed me financially. I shouldn't be struggling to pay my bills. I should be able to help my family members. He should have granted me favor. My struggles should be few. My joys should be many. He should have fought my battles. He should have rebuked the enemy and stayed the hand of the adversary. He should have smiled on my family. My siblings should be saved. My parents should be in good health. My children should be delivered. He should have blessed me abundantly. I shouldn't have struggles in my flesh or lack in my life. But when God does not behave like the good fairy that we want, the enemy exacerbates our problem with believing God. Herein, however, is God glorified: Our faith must lift us to a point where it does not matter what God does, as long as I'm in His will. We must believe that God loves us; and we must embrace His word that says, *"Surely there is an end; and thine expectation shall not be cut off"* (Proverbs 23:18). So whether I go or come; rise up or sit down; remain in the field or go to the city; my expectation is that God is working things out on my behalf (Deuteronomy 28:3).

1. Describe/identify a recent incident when you made an excuse for not doing something that you knew was right to do.

_____

_____

_____

_____

_____

2. Describe/identify a recent incident when you shared or testified to others something that you had prayed about, but the outcome was not as you had hoped. What did you do when confronted by others about your testimony? Did you feel the need to make an excuse for why God didn't honor your request?

_____

_____

_____

_____

_____

3. The next time you are presented with the opportunity to make an excuse for your own behavior or to try and justify why God didn't honor your request, how will you respond?

_____

_____

_____

_____

_____

4. After taking some time to pray and study God's word, write an expectation that you once had, but now realize that it was not aligned with God's will.

_____

_____

_____

_____

_____

5. What steps will you take to ensure that your faith is increased with respect to your expectations and hope?

_____

_____

_____

_____

_____

CHAPTER 8

FROM PROBLEMS
TO PROMISE

But without faith, it is impossible to please God...

(Hebrews 11:6)

Since the days of Adam, God has delivered His people from
bondage to freedom; from prisons to palaces; from death to
life; from sin to redemption; and from problems to promise.
The common elements for those deliverances were faith and
obedience, and the same holds true today. **"Belief" is still the
prescriptive solution for receiving the blessings and the
promises of God.** Conversely, not believing is destined to yield
a life riddled with problems. The problems may come now –
or in the world to come – but for the non-believer, problems

will ultimately come. For the Bible says, "the unbelieving … shall have their part in the lake which burneth with fire and brimstone" (Revelation 21:8).

The joy in believing God is not just founded in the ancillary things that come along with believing. Joy is not predicated on the promise of houses, land, wealth, and riches. Real joy is based on the promise of the status that we achieve when we please God. "But as many as received him, to them gave he power to become the sons of God, even to them that believe on his name" (John 1:12). And when God elevates us to "son-ship," He causes us to be at peace with our enemies; He causes our hearts to seek Him only; He causes our will to be hidden in His; and He causes all things to work together for our good.

The journey from problem to promise is not one that we are expected to navigate on our own. Because Jesus promised to be with us always, we should take courage in knowing that He is with us, even when we are weak in the faith. The beauty in His being with us is that not only does He give us a solution for increasing our faith, but He has a vested interested in seeing us walk into our individual promises. God Himself teaches us how to access those promises. Just as a parent would never tell a child to go ride his bicycle without ensuring that the child knew how to ride; so it is with God. When He commands us to have faith, He's really commanding us to recognize what He has already given us.

It is the trick of the enemy to distract us from what God has placed before us. Our flesh gets in the way. The devil wages war in our minds. Life happens. Fear overwhelms us. Anxiety shakes us. Confusion bewilders us. Excuses overtake us. But it is my prayer that the Holy Spirit will empower you from this day forward to walk in favor, authority, confidence, and expectation.

The promise of being exalted to the status of a son or daughter of God is the true reward of our faith. **"Believing" is our only avenue back to a redemptive relationship with God.** *"If thou shalt confess with thy mouth the Lord Jesus, and shalt believe in thine heart that God hath raised him from the dead, thou shalt be saved"* (Romans 10:9).

As it was in the days of Adam, Abraham, Isaac, and Jacob; the same is true today: **Only those who dare to believe God will ever learn to please God!**

BENEDICTION

If you can admit that your life today does not please God, I invite you to confess your sins, believe in your heart through faith that Jesus is the resurrected Son of God and be saved.

I recognize that there may be some readers who question the very existence of God. For you, I pray that this book challenges you to examine the cause of your disbelief; and I am prayerful that it will invite further dialogue that gives you more insight as to why the believer believes as he does.

If you do have a personal relationship with Jesus as Lord of your life, I invite you to take greater charge of your own life and increase your faith today by affirming that you will actively renounce – and no longer – walk in fear, anxiety, confusion, and excuses. And I agree with you according to Matthew 18:19 that the Holy Spirit will strengthen and increase your awareness that you walk in favor, authority, confidence, and expectation; and lead you from problems to promise!

I pray God's richest blessings upon your life; and as your life is enriched, I pray that: "The Lord bless thee, and keep thee: The

Lord make his face shine upon thee, and be gracious unto thee: The Lord lift up his countenance upon thee, and give thee peace" (Numbers 6:24-26).

If this book has been a blessing to you in any manner, please let me hear from you. I would love to hear your testimonies about how your faith is increased; and if, perhaps, you are interested in scheduling me for speaking engagements, conferences, workshops, or book signings – or for more information about me or my other works – please visit my web site at www.gbcutler.com.

NOTES